the world of ERIC CARLE

THE VERY HUNGRY CATERPILLAR™
Cookbook & Cookie Cutters Kit

Recipes ... v

Carden

chronicle books · san francisco

ISBN 978-1-4521-2552-7

Manufactured in China.

Book design by Ryan Hayes.
Typeset in Gill Sans.

M&M's is a registered trademark of Mars, Incorporated.

10 9 8 7 6 5 4 3 2 1

Chronicle Books LLC
680 Second Street
San Francisco, CA 94107
www.chroniclekids.com

Contents

Food Fun & Kitchen Safety with The Very Hungry Caterpillar™

- The Very Hungry Caterpillar knows that it is important to eat lots of different kinds of foods, including meat, cheese, bread, fresh fruits, and vegetables!

- Measuring, mixing, stirring, sprinkling, spreading—these skills are easy to learn.

- Experiment with different kinds of cheese in the omelets, add lots of different vegetables to the lettuce cups, and try different fruit in your fruit salad each time you make it.

- Try new foods you've never had before. If you don't like them at first—try again!

- Try not to waste food.

- Shop for fruits and vegetables that are fresh and in season.

- Store all your ingredients well so they'll stay fresh and taste their best.

- Never cook without a grown-up and always ask for help using knives, appliances, the stovetop, and the oven.

- You'll need help getting things off high shelves, too.

- Roll up your sleeves, never run in the kitchen, and clean up spills on the floor right away.

- Eat healthful food every day and save sweet treats for special occasions. Otherwise, you might get a tummy ache—just like The Very Hungry Caterpillar did!

Good Morning Eggy Toast

The warm sun comes up and shines its bright rays on The Very Hungry Caterpillar. You might like to begin your day with a sunny breakfast, too!

ingredients

4 slices wheat bread

2 tablespoons butter, at room temperature

4 eggs

2 tablespoons milk

½ cup (55 grams) shredded Cheddar cheese

Salt and pepper

 Butter both sides of the bread slices. Using the caterpillar and butterfly cookie cutters, cut one shape out of the center of each bread slice. In a medium bowl, mix the eggs, milk, and cheese. Season with salt and pepper.

 Heat a large skillet over medium heat. Place 2 bread slices with holes in the pan and cook for 1 minute. Gently fill each hole with one-quarter of the egg mixture. Cook for 2 minutes, until bread is golden and egg is set. Flip carefully with a spatula, and cook for 2 minutes more, until the other side is toasted. Repeat with the remaining 2 bread slices and the remaining egg mixture.

 Place the cutout pieces of bread in the skillet and cook for 4 to 5 minutes, turning once, until browned. Serve warm, accenting the eggy toast with the cutout pieces.

Man in the Moon Pies

Makes 12 pies

In the light of a smiling moon, The Very Hungry Caterpillar's story begins. You might smile as well when you taste these Man in the Moon Pies!

ingredients

Cookies

2½ cups (320 grams) all-purpose flour

1½ teaspoons baking soda

½ teaspoon salt

4 tablespoons (55 grams) unsalted butter, room temperature

4 tablespoons (50 grams) vegetable shortening, room temperature

1 cup (200 grams) light brown sugar, packed

1 egg

1 teaspoon vanilla extract

1¼ cups (300 milliliters) milk

Filling

1⅓ cups (135 grams) confectioners' sugar

½ cup (50 grams) cocoa powder

4 tablespoons (55 grams) unsalted butter, room temperature

3 tablespoons heavy cream

1 teaspoon vanilla extract

½ teaspoon salt

Continued ●—→

To make the cookies: Preheat the oven to 375°F/190°C. Line two baking sheets with parchment paper. Using a 3-inch (7.5-centimeter) round cookie cutter or jar lid, trace circles onto the pieces of parchment, then flip the parchment over so the marked circles are facing the bottom of the baking sheet. You should have 24 circles, 12 on each baking sheet.

 Sift together the flour, baking soda, and salt onto a sheet of wax paper. Using an electric mixer on low speed, beat together the butter, shortening, and light brown sugar in a large bowl until just combined. Increase the speed to medium and beat until fluffy and smooth, about 3 minutes. Add the egg and vanilla and beat until smooth, about 2 minutes. Add half of the flour mixture and half of the milk to the batter and beat on low until just incorporated. Scrape down the sides of the bowl. Add the remaining flour mixture and the remaining milk and beat until completely combined.

 Fit a pastry bag with a #10 round tip and fill the bag with the batter. Trace a circle you made on the parchment with the batter, then fill in the middle. Repeat with the remaining circles and batter until both baking sheets are full.

 Place one baking sheet at a time into the oven and bake for about 10 minutes, or until the cookies spring back when pressed gently. Let the cookies cool on the baking sheet for 5 minutes, then transfer to a baking rack to cool completely.

To make the filling: Using an electric mixer on low speed, beat together the confectioners' sugar, cocoa, and butter in a large bowl until just combined, for about 2 minutes. Increase the speed to medium and beat until crumbly, about 1 minute. Add the cream, vanilla, and salt, increase the speed to high, and beat until smooth, about 3 minutes.

 Using an offset spatula, spread the flat side of one cookie with the filling and top with another cookie. Repeat with the remaining cookies and serve.

Caterpillar Cupcakes

Makes 12 cupcakes

Celebrate with a Caterpillar Cupcake just like The Very Hungry Caterpillar!

ingredients

Cupcakes

1½ cups (185 grams) all-purpose flour

1½ teaspoons baking powder

Dash of salt

½ cup (115 grams) butter, room temperature

1 cup (200 grams) granulated sugar

2 eggs

1 teaspoon vanilla extract

½ cup (120 milliliters) milk

Frosting

¾ cup (170 grams) butter, at room temperature

3 cups (300 grams) confectioners' sugar, plus
more if needed

1½ tablespoons milk, plus more if needed

1½ teaspoons vanilla extract

Red food coloring

Green food coloring

Decorations

2 yellow M&M's

2 green M&M's

12 chocolate chips

1 purple chenille stem or pipe cleaner for the
antennae (from local craft store)

Continued

To make the cupcakes: Preheat the oven to 350°F/180°C.
Line a 12-cup muffin tin with cupcake liners.

 In a medium bowl, combine the flour, baking powder, and salt.
Using an electric mixer on medium speed, cream the butter and
granulated sugar together in a large bowl until light and fluffy, about
5 minutes. Add the eggs, one at a time, and beat until combined.
Add the vanilla and mix until incorporated. Reduce the speed to
low, add one-third of the milk, and mix until combined. Add one-
third of the flour mixture and mix until combined. Repeat, adding
the milk and then the flour mixture, two more times. Mix the batter
for 1 more minute, until completely combined.

 Fill each cupcake liner with the batter until it's about three-fourths full.

 Bake the cupcakes for 15 to 17 minutes, until a cake tester inserted
in the center comes out clean. Let the cupcakes cool for 10 minutes in the tin, then transfer to a baking rack to cool completely.

 To make the frosting: Using an electric mixer on medium speed, beat
the butter in a large bowl until fluffy, about 5 minutes. Add 1½ cups
(150 grams) confectioners' sugar and mix until incorporated. Add
1 tablespoon milk and mix until incorporated. Repeat, adding the
remaining 1½ cups (150 grams) confectioners' sugar and the remaining ½ tablespoon milk. Add the vanilla and beat the frosting for
5 minutes more, until light and fluffy. If the frosting is too stiff, add
½ tablespoon of milk, until it is spreading consistency. If the frosting
is too thin, add more confectioners' sugar, one tablespoon at a time,
until it is spreading consistency.

Move 2 tablespoons of frosting to a small bowl. Add 2 or 3 drops red food coloring and stir together until uniform in color. Add 5 or 6 drops green food coloring to the remaining frosting and stir together until uniform in color.

 To frost and decorate the cupcakes: Frost one cupcake with the red frosting for the caterpillar's head. Press the yellow M&M's into the center of the cupcake to make the eyes. With a toothpick, place a small bit of frosting onto each yellow M&M and then top each with one green M&M, so that they look like pupils. Press one chocolate chip below the eyes to make a nose. Frost the remaining 11 cupcakes with the green frosting.

 Arrange the cupcakes into a caterpillar shape, with the red cupcake at one end, followed by the green cupcakes in an up-and-down curve pattern. Add chocolate chip feet to the bottoms of the green cupcakes. Bend the chenille stem into antennae, cut to desired length, and stick into the red cupcake at the top, above the M&M eyes. Be sure to remove the stem before serving.

Smiling Sun Cookies

Makes 4 dozen cookies

These tangy lemon cookies will brighten your day as bright as the yellow sun in The Very Hungry Caterpillar!

ingredients

Cookies

3 cups (380 grams) all-purpose flour, plus more for work surface

¼ teaspoon salt

2 teaspoons baking powder

I cup (225 grams) butter, room temperature

I cup (200 grams) granulated sugar

Grated zest of I lemon

I egg

I teaspoon vanilla extract

Yellow food coloring

Icing

4 egg whites

2 teaspoons fresh lemon juice

2 teaspoons vanilla extract

6 cups (600 grams) confectioners' sugar, plus more as needed

Yellow food coloring

Continued →

To make the cookies: Preheat the oven to 350°F/180°C.

 In a medium bowl, combine the flour, salt, and baking powder. Using an electric mixer on medium speed, cream the butter, granulated sugar, and lemon zest together in a large bowl until light and fluffy, about 5 minutes. Add the egg, vanilla, and 5 or 6 drops of food coloring and mix until just combined. Add the flour mixture in thirds, mixing until just combined after each addition.

 Turn the dough out onto a floured work surface and knead a few times until smooth. Divide the dough into 2 pieces. Roll out 1 piece of dough until it's ⅛ inch (4 millimeters) thick, sprinkling with flour as needed. Using a 3-inch (7-centimeter) round cookie cutter, cut into the dough to make suns. Repeat with the remaining piece of dough.

Place the cookies on an ungreased baking sheet about 1 inch (2.5 centimeters) apart. Bake for 7 to 9 minutes, until lightly golden. Transfer the cookies to a baking rack to cool completely. Repeat with the remaining cookies.

 To make the icing: Using an electric mixer on high speed, beat the egg whites in a large bowl until they are foamy, about 5 minutes. Add the lemon juice and vanilla and beat until soft peaks form, 3 to 4 minutes. Reduce the speed to medium, gradually add the confectioners' sugar, and beat until the icing is stiff and fluffy, 4 to 5 minutes. Add 6 or 8 drops yellow food coloring and mix at medium speed until uniform in color, 1 to 2 minutes. If the icing is too stiff, add water, ½ teaspoon at a time, until it is piping consistency. If the icing is too thin, add more confectioners' sugar, 1 tablespoon at a time, until it is piping consistency.

 To ice the cookies: Icing hardens very quickly, so cover the bowl with a damp kitchen or paper towel while you are working. Fit a pastry bag with a #3 tip and fill the bag with the icing. Outline the edges of the cookies with the icing. Allow the icing to dry to the touch, about 20 minutes. Remove about three fourths of the icing to a small bowl and thin it with 2 or 3 teaspoons of water. To test the consistency, drop some of the icing back into the bowl. If it disappears within 5 to 10 seconds, it's ready to use. Fill another pastry bag with the thinner icing and cut out a 1/16-inch (2 millimeter) hole from the tip. Fill the outline with the thinned icing. Pop any air bubbles with a toothpick, and gently wiggle the cookie back and forth on a flat surface to settle any lines or ridges. Let the base icing set for 2 to 3 hours. Using the thicker icing, pipe on facial features and rays of sunshine. Allow the icing to dry for 12 to 24 hours before packaging or serving.

Sweet & Spicy Apple Scones

Makes 12 scones

The Very Hungry Caterpillar ate his way through a bright red apple. Here's an apple treat for you to try: yummy apple scones!

ingredients

2½ cups (320 grams) all-purpose flour, plus more for hands, work surface, and cookie cutter

½ cup (40 grams) rolled oats

⅓ cup (65 grams) brown sugar, firmly packed

2½ teaspoons baking powder

½ teaspoon baking soda

½ teaspoon salt

¾ cup (170 grams) unsalted butter, cold

1 large green apple, cored, peeled, and diced

1 cup (240 milliliters) milk, plus 1 tablespoon

2 tablespoons granulated sugar

1 teaspoon cinnamon

 Preheat the oven to 400°F/200°C. Lightly grease a baking sheet.

 Using an electric mixer on medium speed, mix the flour, oats, brown sugar, baking powder, baking soda, and salt in a large bowl until just combined. Slice the butter into 1-tablespoon pieces and distribute over the flour mixture. Mix on low speed until the mixture resembles coarse meal, about 3 to 4 minutes. Add the apple and mix until combined. Add the 1 cup (240 milliliters) milk and mix until the dough holds together.

 With floured hands, divide the dough into 2 pieces and shape into 2 balls. Pat one of the balls until it's ½ inch (12 millimeters) thick on a floured work surface. Using the caterpillar or butter-fly cookie cutter, cut into the dough, dipping the cookie cutter into flour between cuts. Gather the scraps of dough, shape into a ball, and pat until it's ½ inch (12 millimeters) thick. Continue cutting into shapes. Transfer the scones to the prepared baking sheet. Repeat with the remaining ball of dough. You should have 12 scones.

Bake for 12 to 15 minutes, until the scones are dry to the touch and golden.

 While the scones are baking, mix the remaining 1 tablespoon milk with the granulated sugar and cinnamon in a small bowl.

 Brush the scones with the milk mixture while still hot on the pan. Transfer the scones to a rack and let them cool for 5 to 8 minutes. Serve warm or at room temperature.

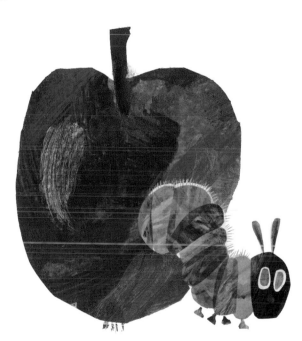

Pear Snacks with Yogurt Dip

A pear is one of The Very Hungry Caterpillar's favorite snacks. But even more fun is a pear slice dipped in sweetened yogurt. Try it!

ingredients

1 cup (240 milliliters) vanilla yogurt

2 tablespoons brown sugar

½ teaspoon cinnamon, plus more for sprinkling

1 teaspoon fresh orange juice

3 ripe pears, cored and sliced lengthwise into
   8 slices

 In a small bowl, stir together the yogurt, sugar, cinnamon, and orange juice until combined. Chill for about 15 minutes before serving.

 For a thicker dip, place a fine-mesh strainer lined with cheesecloth or a coffee filter over a medium bowl. Fill the lined strainer with the yogurt mixture. Chill in the refrigerator overnight. Discard the liquid in the bowl, scrape the thickened dip into a serving bowl, and sprinkle with cinnamon. Serve chilled and dip with pears.

Plum Jam After-School Snacks

Plums are a delicious and healthful treat for you and The Very Hungry Caterpillar! And homemade plum jam is a very special treat because you made it yourself!

ingredients

6 large plums

1½ cups (300 grams) sugar

½ cup (120 milliliters) water

1 tablespoon fresh lemon juice

4 slices sturdy white or wheat bread

special equipment

1-quart (960-milliliter) jar

 To peel the plums, bring a medium stockpot of water to a boil. Fill a large bowl with ice water and have it ready. Using a slotted spoon, gently place the plums one at a time into the boiling water. Let them simmer for 1 minute, then remove them with the slotted spoon and place in the ice water. When the plums are cool to the touch, after about 6 to 7 minutes, remove them from the water and pat dry. Using a small, sharp knife, make a small cut at the top of the plum, near the stem. Stick the tip of the knife into the cut and peel back a strip of the skin. Continue until the plums are all peeled. Then, cut the plums in half and remove the pits.

 Combine the peeled and pitted plums, sugar, water, and lemon juice in a large, heavy stockpot. Cook over medium-low heat until the plums have broken down and the mixture is thick, 15 to 20 minutes, skimming the foam off the top with a spoon as needed. Let the jam cool completely in the pan, then transfer to the jar and refrigerate for up to 1 week.

 Using the caterpillar or butterfly cookie cutters, cut the bread into shapes. Toast and spread with the jam.

Strawberry Shortcake Stacks

 Makes 8 shortcakes

Bright red strawberries, dollops of whipped cream, and tender shortcakes: a delicious dessert or snack. Make these treats in the summer when the strawberries are fresh and ripe!

ingredients

1½ cups (185 grams) all-purpose flour, plus more for work surface, hands, and cookie cutter

⅓ cup (65 grams) sugar, plus 2 teaspoons for strawberries and 1½ tablespoons for whipped cream

1 teaspoon baking powder

½ teaspoon baking soda

½ teaspoon salt

¾ cup (170 grams) unsalted butter, cold

½ cup (120 milliliters) milk

16 large strawberries, hulled and sliced

1½ cups (360 milliliters) heavy cream, cold

 Preheat the oven to 400°F/200°C. Lightly grease a baking sheet.

 Using an electric mixer on medium speed, mix the flour, the ⅓ cup sugar, baking powder, baking soda, and salt until just combined. Slice the butter into 1 tablespoon pieces and distribute over the flour mixture. Mix on low speed until the mixture resembles coarse meal, about 3 to 4 minutes. Add the milk and mix until the dough holds together.

 On a floured work surface, with floured hands, divide the dough into 2 pieces and shape into 2 balls. Pat one of the balls until it's ½ inch (12 millimeters) thick. Using the butterfly or caterpillar cookie cutter, cut into the dough, dipping the cookie cutter into flour between cuts. Gather the scraps of dough, shape into a ball, and pat until it's ½ inch (12 millimeters) thick. Continue cutting into shapes. Transfer the shortcakes to the prepared baking sheet. Repeat with the remaining ball of dough. You should have 8 shortcakes.

 Continued

Bake for 12 to 15 minutes, until the shortcakes are lightly browned and dry to the touch. Transfer the shortcakes to a baking rack to cool completely.

 While the shortcakes are baking, sprinkle the 2 teaspoons sugar over the strawberries in a medium bowl and stir gently to combine. Set aside until the shortcakes cool.

 Just before serving, whip the heavy cream. Using an electric mixer on medium speed, whip the heavy cream until lightly thickened, about 2 minutes. Increase the speed to medium-high and whip until stiff peaks form, about 3 minutes. Add the remaining 1½ tablespoons sugar and beat for 30 seconds, until just combined.

 To serve, split each of the shortcakes in half lengthwise. Dollop half of the whipped cream over the bottom halves of the shortcakes. Spoon the strawberries over the whipped cream, reserving 8 slices for garnish. Cover with the top halves of the shortcakes. Dollop the remaining whipped cream over each shortcake and garnish with a strawberry slice. Serve at once.

Rise & Shine Orange Smoothie

On Friday, The Very Hungry Caterpillar ate through five oranges. But any day of the week is a great day for a Rise & Shine Orange Smoothie!

ingredients

2 cups (480 milliliters) fresh orange juice

1 large, ripe banana, sliced and frozen

1 cup (240 milliliters) vanilla yogurt

1 thin slice of orange, cut crosswise from the center and into quarters, for garnish

 Using a blender on medium speed, blend the orange juice, banana, and yogurt until smooth, about 1 minute. Pour into four small chilled glasses.

 Make one cut in each slice of orange, from the center through the rind. Set the cut of the orange over the edge of the glass to garnish. Serve immediately.

Watermelon Pops

Watermelon is even more fun and refreshing to eat Popsicle-style!

ingredients

Eight ¾-inch (2-centimeter) wedges seedless watermelon

8 gummy worm candies

special equipment

8 Popsicle sticks

 Using the small round cookie cutter, cut a hole in the center of each watermelon wedge.

 Insert 1 Popsicle stick about 1 inch (2.5 centimeters) into each watermelon wedge. Thread 1 gummy worm through the hole in each watermelon wedge.

 Refrigerate the watermelon pops for at least 1 hour or up to overnight. Serve chilled.

Apple Berry Punch

Serves 8

A delicious blend of The Very Hungry Caterpillar's two favorite fruits swirled together in this sparkling drink!

ingredients

16 large strawberries, hulled

4 cups (960 milliliters) sparkling apple cider

 Using a blender on medium speed, blend the strawberries and 1 cup (240 milliliters) cider until smooth, about 1 minute.

 Transfer the strawberry mixture and the remaining 3 cups (720 milliliters) cider to a large pitcher and stir until combined. Serve over ice.

The Very Hungry Caterpillar™ Fruit Salad

The Very Hungry Caterpillar eats a lot of different fruits, one at a time. You can enjoy bite-size pieces of this fruit salad while you read along with or listen to the story!

ingredients

1 apple, cored, peeled, and cut into bite-size pieces

2 pears, cored and cut into bite-size pieces

3 plums, pitted and cut into bite-size pieces

4 strawberries, hulled and quartered

5 oranges, peeled, sectioned, and cut into bite-size pieces

6 to 12 fresh mint leaves

1 In a large bowl, combine the apple, pears, plums, strawberries, and oranges. Refrigerate for at least 30 minutes or up to 6 hours before serving.

2 Serve cold in small bowls garnished with 1 or 2 mint leaves.

Chocolate Mini Cakes

Make your own yummy chocolate cake just like the one The Very Hungry Caterpillar eats!

ingredients

Cakes

2 cups (255 grams) all-purpose flour

2 cups (400 grams) granulated sugar

¾ cup (75 grams) cocoa powder

2 teaspoons baking soda

1 teaspoon baking powder

½ teaspoon salt

1 cup (240 milliliters) brewed coffee, room temperature

1 cup (240 milliliters) milk

½ cup (120 milliliters) vegetable oil

2 teaspoons vanilla extract

2 eggs, lightly beaten

Chocolate Frosting

½ cup (115 grams) butter, room temperature

2 cups (200 grams) confectioners' sugar, plus more as needed

4 tablespoons (60 milliliters) milk, heavy cream, or buttermilk, plus more as needed

2 ounces (55 grams) unsweetened chocolate, melted and cooled to room temperature

1 teaspoon vanilla extract

8 cherries

To make the cakes: Preheat the oven to 350°F/180°C. Grease and flour a 13-by-9-inch (33-by-23-centimeter) baking pan.

 In the bowl of a standing mixer fitted with the whisk or paddle, combine the flour, granulated sugar, cocoa powder, baking soda, baking powder, and salt. In a medium bowl, whisk together the coffee, milk, oil, vanilla, and eggs. With the mixer running on low speed, gradually pour the coffee mixture into the flour mixture and mix just until combined. Continue mixing 2 minutes more, until completely combined. Transfer the batter to the prepared pan.

 Bake the cake for 30 to 35 minutes, until a cake tester inserted in the center comes out clean. Let the cake cool in the pan for 15 minutes, then turn onto a baking rack to cool completely.

 To make the chocolate frosting: Using an electric mixer on medium speed, beat the butter in a large bowl until fluffy, about 5 minutes. Add one-quarter of the confectioners' sugar and mix until incorporated. Add 1 tablespoon milk and mix until incorporated. Repeat, adding one-quarter of the sugar and 1 tablespoon milk, three more times. Add the melted chocolate and vanilla and beat the frosting for 5 minutes more, until light and fluffy. If the frosting is too stiff, add 1 tablespoon of milk at a time, until it is spreading consistency. If the frosting is too thin, add confectioners' sugar, 1 tablespoon at a time, until it is spreading consistency.

Continued

Place the cooled cake on a work surface. Spread the chocolate frosting evenly over the cake, and cut into 8 pieces. To serve, top each cake slice with a cherry and place on a platter.

Ice Cream Cone Surprise

Even The Very Hungry Caterpillar might enjoy this fun lunch surprise!

ingredients

8 eggs, hard-boiled and finely chopped

½ celery stalk, finely chopped

¼ small red onion, finely chopped

2 teaspoons mustard

½ cup (120 grams) mayonnaise

Red food coloring

6 flat-bottom ice cream cones

 In a large bowl, stir together the eggs, celery, onion, and mustard. In a small bowl, stir together the mayonnaise and a few drops of food coloring until uniform in color. Add the mayonnaise to the egg mixture and stir until just combined.

 Scoop the egg salad into the cones with an ice cream scoop. Serve immediately.

Garden Pickles

Make your own pickles! You might even like to design and draw your own pickle jar label or tag!

Makes one 1-quart (680-gram) jar

ingredients

1 pound (455 grams) cucumbers

½ teaspoon dill seeds

½ teaspoon peppercorns

1 cup (240 milliliters) apple cider vinegar

½ cup (120 milliliters) water

½ cup (100 grams) sugar

2 tablespoons salt

Dill leaves (optional)

special equipment

One 1-quart (960-milliliter) jar

 Wash the cucumbers and slice into spears. Place the dill seeds and peppercorns in the bottom of the jar. Pack the cucumber spears into the jar.

 In a large stockpot, bring the vinegar, water, sugar, and salt to a simmer. Pour the vinegar mixture over the cucumbers and into the jar, leaving ½ inch (12 millimeters) of space at the top of the jar. Cover jar with lid and let cool to room temperature.

 Refrigerate for at least 2 days before eating. Store up to 2 months. If desired, garnish with dill leaves when serving.

Tasty Salami Pockets : Serves 8

These savory salami treats are great to pack in a lunchbox or picnic basket, or to eat at home on a rainy day spent reading your favorite book!

ingredients

3 cups (380 grams) all-purpose flour, plus more for the work surface

2 teaspoons salt

1½ teaspoons active dry yeast

1 cup (240 milliliters) lukewarm water

2 tablespoons olive oil, plus more for the bowl and the pan

1 cup (115 grams) shredded mozzarella cheese

16 slices salami

 In a large bowl, stir together the flour, salt, and yeast. Add the lukewarm water and olive oil and stir until it's as mixed as can be—there will still be some floury clumps.

 Turn the dough out onto a floured work surface and knead for 1 to 2 minutes, until a smooth ball forms. Wipe clean and lightly oil the bowl and transfer the dough back to the bowl. Turn the dough inside the bowl so that all sides are coated with oil, then cover the bowl with plastic wrap and a kitchen towel. Let the dough rise in a warm, dark place until doubled in size, about 2 hours.

 Turn the dough back out onto the floured work surface and press it gently to remove the air. (To make ahead, wrap the dough tightly in plastic wrap and refrigerate for up to 1 week. Bring to room temperature before using.) Cover the dough with plastic wrap and a kitchen towel and let rest for 15 minutes. Preheat the oven to 450°F/230°C. Have ready a lightly-greased 15-by-10-inch (38-by-25-centimeter) rimmed baking sheet.

Continued ●—➤

Knead the dough a couple more times, until smooth. Roll the dough out until it's 15 by 10 inches (38 by 25 centimeters). Cut the dough into 8 rectangles. Place 2 tablespoons cheese and 2 slices salami on the lower half of each piece of dough with the short side facing you. Fold the dough over the filling and press around the edges with the tines of a fork to seal. Prick the center of the filled pocket 2 or 3 times with the fork.

 Place the filled pockets on the baking sheet and bake for 12 to 15 minutes, until the dough is golden brown. Remove the pockets to a cooling rack. Serve when cool to the touch.

Swiss Cheese & Mushroom Melts

Just like the Swiss cheese that The Very Hungry Caterpillar eats on Saturday, these cheesy mushroom melts will be a delight to snack on any day of the week!

ingredients

4 teaspoons olive oil

¼ small onion, finely chopped

8 mushrooms, finely chopped

4 large flour tortillas

1 cup (115 grams) shredded Swiss cheese

 Heat 2 teaspoons oil in a large skillet over medium heat. Add the onion and cook until translucent, 3 to 5 minutes. Add the mushrooms and cook until tender, about 5 minutes.

 Lay out 2 tortillas on a work surface. Divide the mushroom mixture between the 2 tortillas and sprinkle evenly with the cheese. Cover with the remaining 2 tortillas.

 Wipe out the skillet with a paper towel. Heat 1 teaspoon oil over medium-high heat for 1 to 2 minutes. Place 1 quesadilla in the pan and cook until the bottom is golden brown, 3 to 4 minutes. Flip and cook the second side until it's golden brown, 2 to 3 minutes. Transfer to a cutting board. Heat the remaining 1 teaspoon oil in the skillet and repeat with the remaining quesadilla.

 Using the caterpillar and butterfly cookie cutters, cut the quesadillas. Save the scraps to heat up and toss into soups or salads, or munch on as a snack. Or cut the quesadillas into wedges and cut out holes with the small, round cookie cutter.

Cookie Lollipops

Makes about 3 dozen cookie pops

Decorate cookie pops to look like the lollipop The Very Hungry Caterpillar eats or use cookie cutters to make your own shapes and designs!

ingredients

Cookies

3 cups (380 grams) all-purpose flour, plus more for work surface and dough

¼ teaspoon salt

2 teaspoons baking powder

1 cup (225 grams) butter, room temperature

1 cup (200 grams) granulated sugar

1 egg

1 teaspoon vanilla extract

Icing

2 egg whites

1 teaspoon fresh lemon juice

1 teaspoon vanilla extract

3 cups (300 grams) confectioners' sugar, plus more as needed

Blue food coloring

Yellow food coloring

special equipment

3 dozen Popsicle sticks

 To make the cookies: Preheat the oven to 350°F/180°C.

 In a medium bowl, combine the flour, salt, and baking powder. Using an electric mixer on medium speed, cream the butter and granulated sugar together in a large bowl until light and fluffy, about 5 minutes. Add the egg and vanilla and mix until just combined. Add the flour mixture in thirds, mixing until just combined after each addition.

 Turn the dough out onto a floured work surface and knead a few times until smooth. Divide the dough into two pieces. Roll out one piece of dough until it's ¼ inch (6 millimeters) thick, sprinkling with flour as needed. Using a 3-inch (7-centimeter) round cookie cutter, cut into the dough to make lollipops. Repeat with the remaining piece of dough. Gather the scraps of dough and roll out until ¼ inch (6 millimeters) thick. Continue cutting into circles. Before the cookies are baked, cut out a caterpillar hole from each one with the small round cookie cutter.

Place the cookies on an ungreased baking sheet about 1 inch (2.5 centimeters) apart. Insert one Popsicle stick about ¾ inch (2 centimeters) into each cookie. Bake for 9 to 11 minutes, until lightly golden. Transfer the cookies to a baking rack to cool completely. Repeat with the remaining cookie dough.

 To make the icing: Using an electric mixer on high speed, beat the egg whites in a medium bowl until they are foamy, about 2 to 3 minutes. Add the lemon juice and vanilla and beat until soft peaks form, about 3 to 4 minutes. Gradually add the confectioners' sugar and beat until the icing is stiff and fluffy, about 3 to 4 minutes. If the icing is too stiff, add water, ½ teaspoon at a time, until it is piping consistency. If the icing is too thin, add more confectioners' sugar, 1 tablespoon at a time, until it is piping consistency. To color the icing, remove half of the icing to a small bowl, add 3 to 4 drops of blue food coloring, and stir until uniform in color. Add 3 or 4 drops of yellow food coloring to the remaining frosting and stir until uniform in color.

 To ice the cookie pops: Icing hardens very quickly, so cover the bowls with a damp kitchen or paper towel while you are working. Fit two pastry bags with a round #3 tip and fill each of the bags with one of the colors of icing. Starting on the outside edge of a cookie, pipe the blue icing in a spiral shape until you reach the middle of the cookie. Repeat with the yellow icing right next to the blue on the cookie. Repeat with the remaining cookies. Let the icing set for at least 30 minutes before serving.

Mini Cherry Pies

A delicious sweet treat perfect for a party or a few hungry friends!
They are even more delicious served with vanilla ice cream or a
sprinkling of confectioners' sugar.

ingredients

12 wonton wrappers

1 cup (270 grams) canned cherry pie filling

 Preheat the oven to 350°F/180°C. Spray a 12-cup muffin tin with nonstick cooking spray. Line each cup with 1 wonton wrapper, pressing so that it's snug against the sides of the cup. Fill each wrapper with 1 heaping tablespoon pie filling.

 Bake for 10 to 12 minutes, until the wonton wrappers are golden and the cherry filling is bubbling. Cool the pies in the muffin tin for 15 minutes, then remove to a cooling rack to cool completely.

Sausage & Cheese Scrambled Egg Muffins

These tasty muffins are great for breakfast (or even lunch or dinner)!
Mix in your favorite savory foods from The Very Hungry Caterpillar,
such as sausage and cheese!

ingredients

12 eggs

½ cup milk

¾ cup (85 grams) shredded Cheddar cheese

12 link breakfast sausages, cooked and
finely chopped

 Preheat the oven to 350°F/180°C. Line a 12-cup muffin tin with cupcake liners and spray with nonstick cooking spray.

 In a large bowl, whisk the eggs and milk. Add the cheese and stir until combined.

 Divide the sausage among the cupcake liners. Pour the egg mixture over the sausage until each cup is about two-thirds full.

 Bake the muffins for 20 to 25 minutes, until the eggs are set and golden. Allow the muffins to cool in the pan for 10 minutes. Serve warm or at room temperature.

Cute Cupcakes & Terrific Toppers

Any day of the week, cupcakes are always a treat. Make them even more special with a decorated topper that you can eat!

ingredients

Cupcakes

1½ cups (185 grams) all-purpose flour

1½ teaspoons baking powder

Dash of salt

½ cup (115 grams) butter, room temperature

1 cup (200 grams) granulated sugar

2 eggs

1 teaspoon vanilla extract

½ cup (120 milliliters) milk

Frosting

¾ cup (170 grams) butter, room temperature

3 cups (300 grams) confectioners' sugar, plus more as needed

4 tablespoons (60 milliliters) milk, heavy cream, or buttermilk, plus more as needed

3 ounces (85 grams) unsweetened chocolate, melted and cooled to room temperature

1½ teaspoons vanilla extract

Toppers

12 ounces (340 grams) white baking chips

2 tablespoons vegetable shortening

Food coloring pens (optional; from craft, cake decorating, or specialty gourmet store)

To make the cupcakes: Preheat the oven to 350°F/180°F. Line a 12-cup muffin tin with cupcake liners.

 In a medium bowl, combine the flour, baking powder, and salt. Using an electric mixer on medium speed, cream the butter and granulated sugar together in a large bowl until light and fluffy, about 5 minutes. Add the eggs, one at a time, and beat until combined. Add the vanilla and mix until incorporated. Reduce the speed to low, add one-third of the milk, and mix until combined. Add one-third of the flour mixture and mix until combined. Repeat, adding the milk and then the flour mixture, two more times. Mix the batter for 1 more minute, until completely combined.

 Fill each cupcake liner with the batter until it's about three-fourths full.

 Bake the cupcakes for 15 to 17 minutes, until a cake tester inserted in the center comes out clean. Let the cupcakes cool for 10 minutes in the tin, then transfer to a baking rack to cool completely.

 To make the frosting: Using an electric mixer on medium speed, beat the butter in a large bowl until fluffy, about 5 minutes. Add one-quarter of the confectioners' sugar and mix until incorporated. Add 1 tablespoon milk and mix until incorporated. Repeat, adding one-quarter of the sugar and 1 tablespoon milk, three more times. Add the melted chocolate and vanilla and beat the frosting for 5 minutes more, until light and fluffy. If the frosting is too stiff, add 1 tablespoon of milk, until it is spreading consistency. If the frosting is too thin, add more confectioners' sugar, 1 tablespoon at a time, until it is spreading consistency.

Continued

6 To make the cupcake toppers: Line a baking sheet with parchment paper. Using a 3-inch (7-centimeter) round cookie cutter or jar lid, or the butterfly or caterpillar cookie cutters, trace around the cutters onto the piece of parchment and then flip the parchment over so the marked shapes are facing the bottom of the baking sheet. You should have 12 shapes.

7 Put the white chips and shortening into a medium heatproof bowl and set over a pot of simmering water, making sure the water does not touch the bottom of the bowl. Stir the chips and shortening until melted and smooth.

8 Fit a pastry bag with a #3 round tip and fill the bag with the melted chips. Pipe around the traced shapes with the melted chips. When the candy is set, 5 to 10 minutes, fill in the rest of the shape with melted chips. Refrigerate the cupcake toppers until set, 15 to 20 minutes.

9 Frost the cupcakes with the frosting and top with a cupcake topper. To make it extra-fancy, add details with food coloring pens.

Green Leaf Lettuce Wraps

Makes 12 lettuce cups

The Very Hungry Caterpillar ate through one nice green leaf just before turning into a butterfly. You might like to try these healthful and refreshing lettuce cups!

ingredients

1 large cucumber, peeled, seeded, and chopped into bite-size pieces

25 cherry tomatoes, quartered

2 celery stalks, cut into ½-inch pieces

¼ cup (60 grams) mayonnaise

1 teaspoon fresh lemon juice

12 large butter lettuce leaves

 In a large bowl, combine the cucumber, tomatoes, and celery. Add the mayonnaise and lemon juice and stir until combined.

 To assemble the lettuce cups, fill each lettuce leaf with a generous scoop of the vegetable mixture, roll it up, and eat!

Hot Dog Cocoons

Warm baked bread hot dogs: comfort food that will make you feel
just like the caterpillar wrapped up in his cocoon.

ingredients

3 cups (380 grams) all-purpose flour,
plus more for work surface

2 teaspoons salt

1½ teaspoons active dry yeast

1 cup (240 milliliters) lukewarm water

2 tablespoons olive oil, plus more for the bowl

8 hot dogs

1 egg, beaten

 In a large bowl, stir together the flour, salt, and yeast. Add the lukewarm water and oil and stir until it's as mixed as can be—there will still be some floury clumps.

 Turn the dough out onto a floured work surface and knead for 2 to 3 minutes, until a smooth ball forms. Wipe out the bowl with a paper towel, then lightly oil the inside of the bowl and return the dough to the bowl. Turn the dough inside the bowl so that all sides are coated with oil, then cover the bowl with plastic wrap and a kitchen towel. Let the dough rise in a warm, dark place until doubled in size, about 2 hours.

 Turn the dough back out onto the floured work surface and press it gently to remove the air. (To make ahead, wrap the dough tightly in plastic wrap, refrigerate for up to 1 week, and bring to room temperature before using.) Cover the dough with plastic wrap and a kitchen towel and let rest for 15 minutes. Preheat the oven to 450°F/230°C.

4 Knead the dough a couple more times, until smooth. Roll out the dough until it's 15 by 10 inches (38 by 25 centimeters). Cut the dough into 8 rectangles. Cut each rectangle into 4 strips, lengthwise. Wrap each hot dog with 4 bread dough strips, starting at one end and wrapping the dough, overlapping the strips, until you reach the other end of the hot dog.

5 Place the wrapped hot dogs on the ungreased baking sheet. Brush each cocoon with the egg. Bake for 25 to 30 minutes, until the dough is golden brown. Allow to cool on the pan for about 10 minutes. Serve warm or at room temperature.

Beautiful Butterfly Sandwiches

The Very Hungry Caterpillar turns into a beautiful butterfly! Celebrate any occasion with these beautiful butterfly sandwiches. Not only are they fun to make and eat, they're also perfect for hungry party guests of all ages!

ingredients

8 pieces large sturdy white bread, such as sourdough or potato bread

3 or 4 colors of food coloring

Two 5-ounce (140-gram) cans water-packed tuna

1 celery stalk, finely chopped

¼ onion, finely chopped

1 tablespoon pickle relish

1 egg, hard-boiled and grated

½ cup (120 grams) mayonnaise

 Using the butterfly cookie cutter, cut out 2 butterfly shapes from each slice of bread. Save the scraps for making breadcrumbs or croutons.

 Place several drops of each food coloring into the separate sections of an ice cube tray, mini muffin tin, or several small bowls. Using a small, clean paintbrush (one that hasn't been used for paint or crafts), paint one side of each of the bread shapes with the food coloring. Lightly toast the bread in a toaster or bake it in a 300°F/150°C toaster oven for 5 to 6 minutes to set the color.

 Drain the tuna, place it in a large bowl, and flake it with a fork. Add the celery, onion, relish, egg, and mayonnaise and stir until combined. Fill the sandwiches with the tuna salad and serve immediately.

Bye-Bye Butterfly Fruit Centerpiece

Makes 1 centerpiece

Say "Goodbye" to the butterfly as he flies away at the end of the story. Enjoy this colorful fruit platter and Eric Carle's bright collage illustrations as you begin to read the book again!

ingredients

1 medium banana, peeled and halved lengthwise

4 large strawberries, hulled and thinly sliced, plus 1 large strawberry, hulled and halved*

1 pint blueberries

4 green grapes, sliced in half

4 red grapes, sliced in half

*You'll use only one half of the banana and last strawberry. Save the other halves for a snack or freeze them to use in smoothies!

In the center of a large white platter or serving tray, place one half of the banana cut-side down. Arrange the thinly sliced strawberries, blueberries, and green and red grapes in stripes and swirls in the shape of wings around the banana. Place one half of the last strawberry at the top end of the banana to make the head of the butterfly.